BRAIN ACADEMY Quests

MISSION FILE 4

Richard Cooper and Penny Hollander

Consultant for NACE:
Sue Mordecai

nace

RISING STARS

Rising Stars are grateful to the following people for their support in developing this series:
Julie Fitzpatrick, Johanna Raffan and Belle Wallace

nace

NACE, PO Box 242, Arnolds Way, Oxford, OX2 9FR
www.nace.co.uk

Rising Stars UK Ltd, 22 Grafton Street, London W1S 4EX
www.risingstars-uk.com

Every effort has been made to trace copyright holders and obtain their permission for the use of copyright materials. The authors and publisher will gladly receive information enabling them to rectify any error or omission in subsequent editions.

All facts are correct at time of going to press.

Published 2005
Reprinted 2005, 2007
Text, design and layout © Rising Stars UK Ltd

Editorial Consultant: Sue Mordecai
Design: Hart McLeod
Illustrations: Cover and insides – Sue Lee / Characters – Bill Greenhead
Cover Design: Burville-Riley

All rights reserved. No part of this publication may be reproduced, stored in a retrieval system, or transmitted, in any form by any means, electronic, mechanical, photocopying, recording or otherwise, without the prior permission of Rising Stars.

British Library Cataloguing in Publication Data.
A CIP record for this book is available from the British Library.

ISBN: 978-1-90505-635-4

Printed by Craft Print International Limited, Singapore

CONTENTS

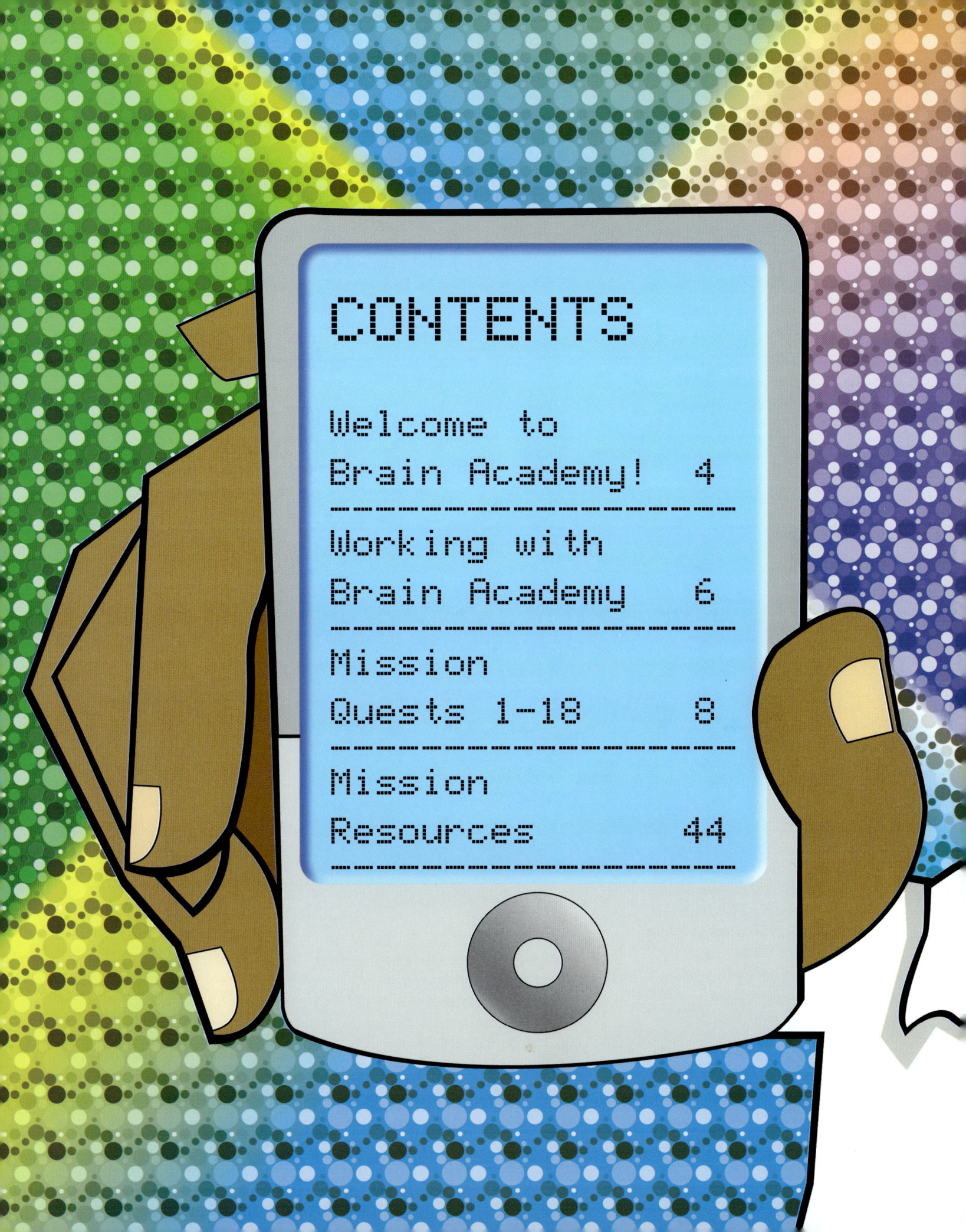

Welcome to
Brain Academy!   4

Working with
Brain Academy   6

Mission
Quests 1-18   8

Mission
Resources   44

Welcome to Brain Academy!

Welcome to Brain Academy! Make yourself at home. We are here to give you the low-down on the organisation — so pay attention!

It's our job to help Da Vinci and his colleagues to solve the tough problems they face and we would like you to join us as members of the Academy. Are you up to the challenge?

Da Vinci
Da Vinci is the founder and head of the Brain Academy. He is all seeing, all thinking and all knowing – possibly the cleverest person alive. Nobody has ever actually seen him in the flesh as he communicates only via computer. When Da Vinci receives an emergency call for help, the members of Brain Academy jump into action (and that means you!).

Huxley
Huxley is Da Vinci's right-hand man. Not as clever, but still very smart. He is here to guide you through the missions and offer help and advice. The sensible and reliable face of Brain Academy, Huxley is cool under pressure.

Dr Hood
The mad doctor is the arch-enemy of Da Vinci and Brain Academy. He has set up a rival organisation called DAFT (which stands for Dull And Feeble Thinkers). Dr Hood and his agents will do anything they can to irritate and annoy the good people of this planet. He is a pain we could do without.

Hilary Kumar
Ms Kumar is the Prime Minister of our country. As the national leader she has a hotline through to the Academy but will only call in an extreme emergency. Confident and strong willed, she is a very tough cookie indeed.

General Cods-Wallop
This highly decorated gentleman (with medals, not wallpaper) is in charge of the armed forces. Most of his success has come from the help of Da Vinci and the Academy rather than the use of his somewhat limited military brain.

Mrs Tiggles
Stella Tiggles is the retired head of the Secret Intelligence service. She is a particular favourite of Da Vinci who treats her as his own mother. Mrs Tiggles' faithful companion is her cat, Bond… James Bond.

We were just like you once — ordinary schoolchildren leading ordinary lives. Then one day we all received a call from a strange character named Da Vinci. From that day on, we have led a double life — as secret members of Brain Academy!

Here are a few things you should know about the people you'll meet on your journey.

Echo the Eco-Warrior
Echo is the hippest chick around. Her love of nature and desire for justice will see her do anything to help an environmental cause – even if it means she's going to get her clothes dirty.

Maryland T Wordsworth
M T Wordsworth is the president of the USA. Not the sharpest tool in the box, Maryland prefers to be known by his middle name, Texas, or 'Tex' for short. He takes great exception to being referred to as 'Mary' (which has happened in the past).

Buster Crimes
Buster is a really smooth dude and is in charge of the Police Force. His laid-back but efficient style has won him many friends, although these don't include Dr Hood or the DAFT agents who regularly try to trick the coolest cop in town.

Sandy Buckett
The fearless Sandy Buckett is the head of the Fire Service. Sandy and her team of brave firefighters are always on hand, whether to extinguish the flames of chaos caused by the demented Dr Hood or just to rescue Mrs Tiggles' cat…

Serena
Serena is a new character to Brain Academy. A time-traveller, Serena knows all about what went on before – and a bit about the future too.

Victor Blastov
Victor Blastov is the leading scientist at the Space Agency. He once tried to build a rocket by himself but failed to get the lid off the glue. Victor often requires the services of the Academy, even if it's to set the video to record Dr Who.

Prince Barrington
Prince Barrington, or 'Bazza' as he is known to his friends, is the publicity-seeking heir to the throne. Always game for a laugh, the Prince will stop at nothing to raise money for worthy causes. A 'good egg' as his mother might say.

5

Working with Brain Academy

Do you get the idea? Now you've had the introduction we are going to show you the best way to use this book.

The Quest
This tells you what the quest is about.

Research Area
Da Vinci will give you some research tips before you start working on the brief.

MISSION QUEST 4:12

Grand designs

The Academy needs livening up. It's looking very drab. Can't we give it a coat of paint?

I've been going to an evening art class, Da Vinci. What about a few pictures instead? We could do something really exciting.

Sounds interesting, Mrs T. Let's get the Academy to help.

The Quest
Your quest is to choose a famous painting and reproduce it on a larger scale for the Brain Academy ballroom. In order to help you decide what might suit the Academy, gather together a collection of art magazines and journals. Ask your teachers or parents for books and postcards which show well-known and less well-known works of art.

Research Area
Start by looking at the National Gallery website at:
http://www.nationalgallery.org.uk
Visit the Tate Gallery at:
http://www.tate.org.uk You can also follow the links to the Tate Modern, Tate Liverpool and Tate St Ives.

There is more information on pages 46–47.

30

Each mission is divided up into different parts.

No one said this was easy. In fact that is why you have been chosen. Da Vinci will only take the best and he believes that includes you. Good luck!

Each book contains a number of 'quests' for you to take part in. You will work with the characters in Brain Academy to complete these quests.

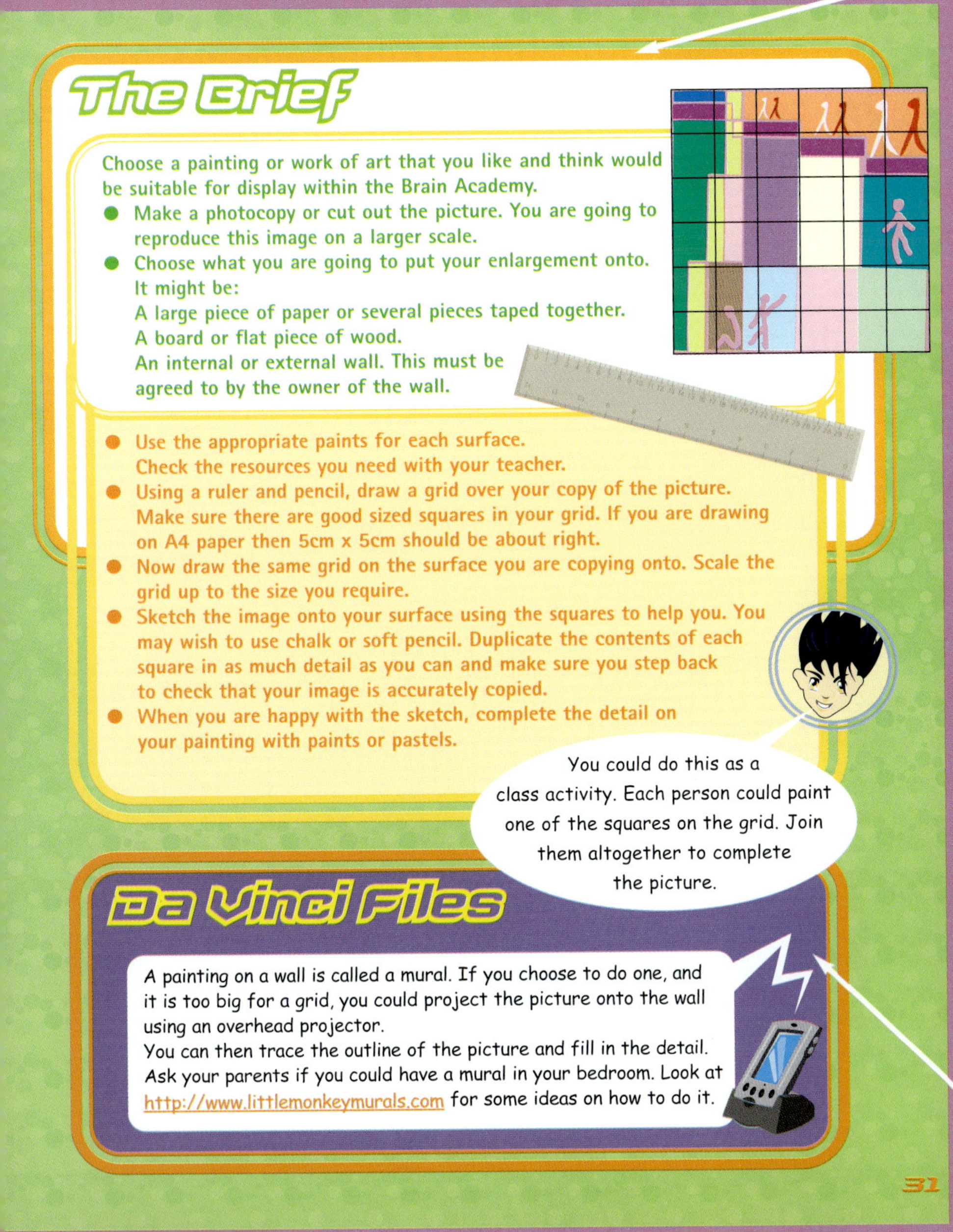

The Brief
This is where you try to complete the challenge.

The Brief

Choose a painting or work of art that you like and think would be suitable for display within the Brain Academy.
- Make a photocopy or cut out the picture. You are going to reproduce this image on a larger scale.
- Choose what you are going to put your enlargement onto. It might be:
A large piece of paper or several pieces taped together.
A board or flat piece of wood.
An internal or external wall. This must be agreed to by the owner of the wall.

- Use the appropriate paints for each surface. Check the resources you need with your teacher.
- Using a ruler and pencil, draw a grid over your copy of the picture. Make sure there are good sized squares in your grid. If you are drawing on A4 paper then 5cm x 5cm should be about right.
- Now draw the same grid on the surface you are copying onto. Scale the grid up to the size you require.
- Sketch the image onto your surface using the squares to help you. You may wish to use chalk or soft pencil. Duplicate the contents of each square in as much detail as you can and make sure you step back to check that your image is accurately copied.
- When you are happy with the sketch, complete the detail on your painting with paints or pastels.

You could do this as a class activity. Each person could paint one of the squares on the grid. Join them altogether to complete the picture.

Da Vinci Files

A painting on a wall is called a mural. If you choose to do one, and it is too big for a grid, you could project the picture onto the wall using an overhead projector.
You can then trace the outline of the picture and fill in the detail. Ask your parents if you could have a mural in your bedroom. Look at http://www.littlemonkeymurals.com for some ideas on how to do it.

31

Da Vinci Files
These problems are for the best Brain Academy recruits. Very tough. Are you tough enough?

PS: See pages 44—47 for a useful process and hints and tips!

7

MISSION QUEST 4:1

School of Rock!

"The Felix School of Rock composed a brilliant song for our annual music celebrations but Dr Hood and his D.A.F.T. agents have destroyed my copy of the tape they sent!"

"I managed to rescue the first part, Bazza. Perhaps the Questers can help us to complete it."

The Quest

Your quest is to complete the song and arrange a performance of Brain Academy Braveheart! You can work in groups and should decide who is going to play which instrument, and who is hoping to sing, in your band.

Research Area

Look at these websites to get some ideas on song writing and instrument backing:

http://www.bbc.co.uk/schools/digger/9_11entry/flash/musicmixer.shtml
http://www.bbc.co.uk/schools/digger/9_11entry/flash/song.shtml
http://pbskids.org/jazz/bandleader.html

There is more information on pages 46–47.

The Brief

First, complete the song lyrics below.

BRAIN ACADEMY BRAVEHEART
There was evil,
Evil all around.
There was danger,
Danger on the ground.

We needed someone,
Someone strong and brave

The next step is to compose a melody and add backing instruments. Finally, notate the parts for each instrument and the melody so your band can perform the song.

Perhaps you could add a descant group to your song. Find a way to write your melody down so other musicians can play it.

Try to include names of the Brain Academy members. Send your song to Brain Academy, Rising Stars, 22 Grafton Street, London W1S 4EX

Da Vinci Files

- Practise the completed song and, if you can, videotape or record a performance.
- Remember that the way you look and move are important too, so make your performance as original and memorable as you can.
- Use any computer software that your school may have to watch and edit your performance.

MISSION QUEST 4:2

Looking at Llandudno

"Huxley, I've been invited to Llandudno, in Wales, to give a lecture on thinking skills. But I'm a bit worried that the street signs will all be in Welsh so I won't be able to find my way around and I'm only there for one day…"

"Calm down, Da Vinci. I've been to Wales before. Pob lwc!"

"Well, Huxley, I'd like to make the most of it and not waste time trying to decide what to do and see…"

"Hmm… I think I feel a plan coming on…"

The Quest

Your quest is to make Da Vinci an easy-to-read guidebook for Llandudno.
Da Vinci won't have much spare time, so you are going to plan his trip for him and choose the attractions he will visit.

Research Area

Look at these websites first:

http://Llandudno-tourism.co.uk
http://maps.google.co.uk

There is more information on pages 46–47.

The Brief

- Locate Llandudno using Google maps, and print off a copy for Da Vinci before you start.
- Go to the Llandudno Tourism website. Find the 'Easy to get to' section and decide how Da Vinci should travel. Write this as an opening page for your guidebook.
- There are three places of interest that Da Vinci should definitely find time for: Conwy Castle; Codman's Punch and Judy, and the Welsh Mountain Zoo. Choose a fourth attraction for Da Vinci and write guidebook entries for all four places.
- Keep your entries brief and use interesting language and illustrations, to persuade Da Vinci that your recommendations are worthwhile. Use report-style (present tense) writing.

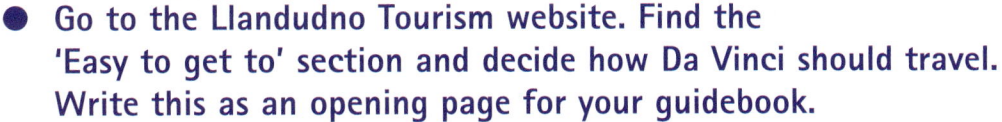

- Make the guidebook by folding two pieces of A4 paper in half. You will have a front and back cover and six pages.
- Put an index on the inside back cover and instructions on how to get to Llandudno on the inside front cover. Use one page for each of your four attractions.
- Stick the map on the back cover, and find an image for the front. Give your guidebook a title.

Can you advise Da Vinci of the order in which he should visit the places of interest? Remember: he has to see them all in one day.

How will you help Da Vinci make sure he pronounces Llandudno, and other Welsh place names correctly?

Da Vinci Files

- Write and record a radio advert promoting Llandudno as a great holiday destination.
- Remember to make the town sound as attractive as possible.
- If you live in or near Llandudno, perhaps you could record interviews with your friends and family about the town, to include in your advert!

MISSION QUEST 4:3

Chocs away!

"Echo, I need your help to make a fantastic chocolate sauce for the Brain Academy supper next week. However, as we are spending too much money on electricity, you must try to save energy and create an ecological choccy sauce!"

"OK, so to save energy we need a mixture that will melt at the lowest possible temperature…"

"I'll leave this in your capable hands, but no eating all the ingredients yourself!"

The Quest

Your quest is to find the mixture of butter and chocolate that will melt quickest. You will need to experiment with different proportions of the ingredients and prepare a recipe that will enable Echo to cook up a storm at the Brain Academy supper!

Research Area

Try these websites to get you started:

http://www.bbc.co.uk/schools/scienceclips/ages/9_10/changing_state.shtml
http://www.exploratorium.edu/cooking/icooks/06-09-03.html
http://www.bbc.co.uk/schools/revisewise/science/materials

There is more information on pages 46–47.

The Brief

You will need:
- Chocolate bars, broken into pieces
- Weighing scales
- Wooden spoon
- Butter
- Bowl
- Oven/hob

- Make up to four mixtures of chocolate and different types of butter or butter substitutes.
- To make your test fair, you should only change one element of the experiment at a time; for example, the oven/hob temperature or the quantity of chocolate to butter.
- When you have reached your conclusion, write a recipe for Echo to follow. Include the weights of the different ingredients and the temperature of the most efficient heat source.

Don't let your mixture boil and keep safe in the kitchen when handling hot mixtures and cookware. Always use protective gloves and stay near your experiment.

Does it make a difference if you use white, milk or dark chocolate? Find out if the production of chocolate is important to any countries.

Da Vinci Files

- Remember, the sauce needs to taste good, as well as being ecologically friendly. Write down a recipe for the rest of the dessert for the Academy supper, so that your chocolate sauce has something to be eaten with! You could invent something new or share your favourite dessert.
- Gather all your recipes together in your class or group and paste them into a scrapbook to make up the Brain Academy Pudding Cookbook.

MISSION QUEST 4:4

My Kingdom for a retreat!

"Da Vinci has asked me to choose the best place to build his holiday retreat, Serena. It needs to be somewhere where he can't be pestered by those pesky D.A.F.T. agents. Needless to say, I haven't a clue…"

"Why not use your military experience and find the most strategically positioned spot, General? Castles were always built in strategic positions."

"I like your style, young lady. Let's get to work!"

The Quest

Your quest is to build a 3D model of a land relief, which includes Da Vinci's holiday home in a strategic position. You will need to research existing castles to review why they were built in their specific locations. If there is a castle near where you live, try to visit it to get first-hand experience of the site.

Research Area

Start by looking at other castle locations around the UK. Try this site:
http://www.castleuk.net

Pictures of a land relief model can be seen at:
www.curator.pwp.blueyonder.co.uk/common.htg/frameh.htm

There is more information on pages 46–47.

Try looking in Railway Modeller magazine for some great landscape models. The N Gauge Society has some good pictures of model railways and scenery on its webpage.

14

The Brief

Carry out your research first: 
- What strategic points do many castles share?
- Why were the castles built where they were?
- Which geographical features made it difficult for invaders?
- Study the following geographical features on a map before making your decision: rivers, hills, coastlines, marshland, roads, railway lines.
- Use an Ordnance Survey map of your local area to choose the best position to build a secure holiday home for Da Vinci.

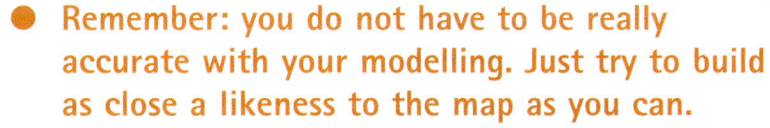

Building the model 
- Remember: you do not have to be really accurate with your modelling. Just try to build as close a likeness to the map as you can.
- Build the model on a solid baseboard.
- Draw a birds-eye view of the relief on the board. Include contours and any water.
- You can use polystyrene tiles cut to shape, papier mâché or modelling clay to build your model.
- Paint your model and add any extras such as trees or farm animals for realism.
- Place Da Vinci's holiday home in the best strategic position. This can be made from matchboxes or a construction kit.

If a permanent model is too hard you could use wet sand in a sand table to model it in relief. Ask for help with difficult modelling skills like cutting and consider the scale of your model.

Da Vinci Files

- Bring your model to life by adding a painted backdrop.
- Name Da Vinci's holiday retreat. Serena says "I like MALMAISON as it is an anagram of my favourite painting!"
- Invent characters who would be Da Vinci's neighbours. You can make them as friendly or as eccentric as you like!

15

MISSION QUESTS/SUPERQUEST 4:5–4:6

Extreme weather

"Tex, it's time we all signed the international treaty to investigate global warming. Our climate seems to be changing so rapidly…"

"You're right Hilary. I need to find out more about the extreme weather conditions we keep seeing around the world."

"I think Tex needs the help of the Academy. Its over to you!"

The Super Quest

Your quest is to make a multimedia presentation for Tex and Hilary Kumar about extreme weather conditions around the world and how they affect the human race. You can use a variety of presentation methods to get your message across. This quest is suitable for pairs or groups, so divide your research evenly between your team-mates.

Research Area

Start by looking at the following websites:

http://www.bbc.co.uk/science/hottopics/naturaldisasters/
http://news.bbc.co.uk/cbbcnews/hi/find_out/guides/world/
    global_warming/newsid_1575000/1575441.stm

Look up news events from 2004-5, such as the Asian Tsunami or Hurricane Katrina which hit New Orleans.

Find out the difference between a hurricane and a tornado.

There is more information on pages 46–47.

The Brief

Your presentation needs to be as clear as possible so everyone can understand your research. You are going to have to use lots of different ways to get your message across. This quest would be suitable for working in pairs or groups. Use a selection of the following methods:
- Charts and graphs
- Film clips from video, DVD or the Internet
- PowerPoint presentations
- Information posters
- Zigzag books
- 3D models
- Illustrated booklets.

CONTINUED ➡

Research the following areas. You may wish to investigate all of them for your presentation or just two or three.
- Hurricanes/typhoons
- Tornados
- Extreme temperatures: heat waves and 'big freezes'
- Extreme rainfall: flooding and its effects
- Lightning strikes: what should you do if you are caught in a thunderstorm?

- Changes in living memory: ask relatives or neighbours of all ages about the climate changes they have noticed since they were children.
- Consider the effects of extreme weather on humans: loss of life, damage to buildings, forest fires, water shortages and financial costs.
- How can we protect ourselves? Investigate evacuating people, tornado shelters, firefighting, flood defences and measures taken by governments and aid agencies such as the Red Cross.

Did you know that one of the safest places to be during an electrical storm is inside a car! Can you find out why?

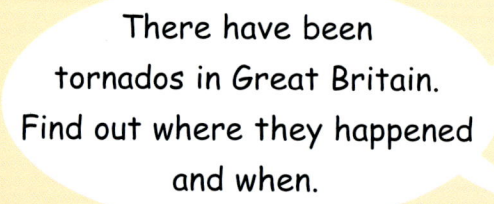

There have been tornados in Great Britain. Find out where they happened and when.

Now give your presentation to your class.

Now you have shown us all about the world's weather, we need to report on how we can affect it. The Earth's climate is changing. Some scientists talk about 'The Greenhouse Effect', 'greenhouse gases' and 'global warming'. Investigate these phrases.
What can we as individuals do to help?
What can governments do to help?
What might happen if we and the other countries of the world do nothing about global warming?

Da Vinci Files

I want you to contact the President of the United States and our Prime Minister.

Draw up an action plan that you think these governments should follow to help stop global warming. It could be a step-by-step plan with bullet points or a letter setting our your views. You need to persuade these world leaders with your arguments.

The President of the United States of America
The White House
1600 Pennsylvania Avenue NW
Washington, DC 20500
USA

The Prime Minister
10 Downing Street
London
SW1A 2AA

Send your plans to these addresses and include your name and the address of your school. See if you get a reply. I'll have words with them myself if you don't!

MISSION QUEST 4:7

Hello! Bonjour! Guten Tag!

"Huxley dear boy, we're hosting the Creative Thinking World Championships next week and you've got to meet and greet all the world's finest minds. How's your French?"

"Tres bien indeed, Da Vinci. It's the rest of the languages I'm worried about!"

"Well you'd better hurry up and learn the basic greetings. We want to make a good impression."

"Aidez-moi, vite!"

The Quest

Your quest is to make a set of flash cards for Huxley to use when he greets the competitors in the Creative Thinking World Championships. Your cards will need to present a series of facts and information in a clear and easy to read format, so do your research carefully.

Research Area

Gather together a collection of atlases, maps, travel guides and books.
Use the language tool feature on Google.
http://www.google.co.uk

There is more information on pages 46–47.

The Brief

This quest is suitable for individuals, groups or classes.

- Make a set of A4 flash cards showing the key words and phrases that are spoken in different countries. The cards can be put in a folder and added to over time. You could index the flash cards or they could form part of a display.
- Each flash card should have the name of the country and its national flag on one side. Start with France, Italy and Germany then add as many other countries from around the world as you wish.
- On the other side, draw or stick in a picture of a famous place or landmark.
- In a grid format set out the key words and phrases in the native language, with the English translation.

Suitable phrases to include are:
- Greetings.
- Questions a traveller to that country may ask.
- A list of foods or dishes that that country is famous for.
- Places that a visitor may wish to go to.
- Trades and industries that the country specialises in.
- Geographical features of the country such as mountains, beaches, rivers, etc.

New words are invented all the time and added to the Oxford English dictionary. See if you can find the most recent additions at http://www.askoxford.com. Are there foreign versions of these words?

See if you can find out what a 'cockerpoo' and a 'labradoodle' are. (They do exist!)

Da Vinci Files

Ask your teachers to help you organise an International Carnival Day.
- You could celebrate the diversities within your school or choose a country to explore in more detail. An Italian, French or Jamaican Day would be fun!
- Make your own national costumes, eat different foods, learn new words and play different music for each country you celebrate.
- You could use this as a way of fundraising for your school by hosting competitions and games.

MISSION QUEST 4:8

Superstructures!

Did you know that the Great Pyramid in Egypt was the tallest building in the world for nearly 4500 years, Da Vinci?

And that a superstructure can be seen from space. Which one is it?

Umm... Of course I did, Serena...

Err, Huxley, where are you? Help!

So do you know which building replaced it as the tallest building in the world?

The Quest

Your quest is to research the history of tall buildings and superstructures. Investigate how they were built and the materials that were used. Present your findings to the class and mark your landmark buildings on a world map. Add all your presentation pages together to make a reference book to add to your class library.

Research Area

Dorling Kindersley publish lots of books about buildings with some great illustrations. See 'Amazing Buildings'.

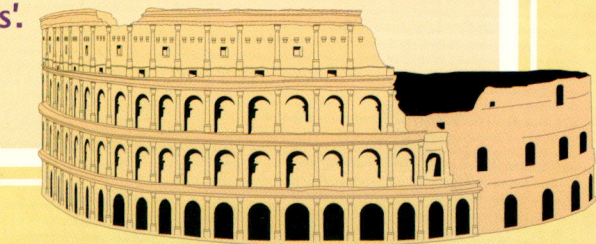

There is more information on pages 46–47.

22

The Brief

Decide which superstructures you want to study and plan your presentation and book.
The contents will depend on what you find out. You could decide on a title such as 'Twelve Superstructures' so that you have a set number to put in the book and divide the research between a pair or group. Include as much information as you can find.

Here are some places to investigate.
- Buildings from Ancient times; the Pyramids, the Colosseum, Celtic hill-forts.
- Great bridges of the world from the first Iron Bridge to the huge suspension bridges such as the Humber Bridge and the Golden Gate Bridge in San Francisco.
- The tallest buildings in the world: Petronas Towers and the Sears Tower.
- The Channel tunnel and other feats of engineering.
- Stonehenge: what was it used for and how could it have been created?
- Extravagant royal palaces like the Brighton Pavilion, the Palace of Versailles in France or the Imperial Palace in the Forbidden City, Beijing.
- Elaborate castles such as Neuschwanstein Castle in Bavaria.
- Ancient and modern sports stadiums like the Circus Maximus in Rome and Wembley Stadium in London or the Millennium Stadium in Cardiff.
- The Opera Houses in Paris and Sydney.
- Unusual designs such as Dubai's Palm Island, the 'Gherkin' in London and the design to replace the World Trade Centre in New York.

The Colosseum in Ancient Rome held mock sea battles with real ships and men. Can you find out more about how this was done?

Da Vinci Files

The Crystal Palace was built for the Great Exhibition in 1851. The Millennium Dome was built to celebrate the beginning of the new millennium. Both really were 'superstructures'.
- Design your own building to celebrate a milestone for your school.
- Draw it from different viewpoints, label it, provide a key and finally name it.

MISSION QUEST 4:9

A watery worry

"We've had so much hot weather lately that some of the riverbeds are more sand than water, Victor! We need to explain to everyone about the water cycle so that they can be more careful about their water consumption."

"Would one of my inventions be of any use, Sandy?"

"Not really, we need to get the message across about why we run out of water first. Let's get the Brain Academy involved and hope it rains soon!"

The Quest

You need to make a classroom display about the water cycle and how evaporation works, so that Victor and other members of the Brain Academy can learn about where we get water from and how valuable a resource it is.

Research Area

Start by looking at these websites:

http://www.environment-agency.gov.uk/commondata/acrobat/communications.pdf
http://www.bbc.co.uk/schools/riverandcoasts/water_cycle/rivers/index.shtml

There is more information on pages 46–47.

The Brief

- Find out as much as you can about how the water cycle works, then plan your display. You can work in groups, each drawing a diagram to show a stage of the process, then write captions in report style (present tense) for each stage. Keep the captions as simple as possible.
- Cut out your diagrams and captions and stick them onto a large piece of coloured paper in the correct order. You should have a large poster with all the cycle stages represented.
- At the bottom of your poster, create a section called REMEMBER! Into this put six key ideas you have researched for saving water in times of drought.

Use imperatives, such as DO, DON'T and THINK in your REMEMBER! section.

Water your garden with a watering can. A watering can uses four litres of water, whereas a sprinkler uses 540 litres per hour!

Da Vinci Files

Now that you know such a lot about water and how to save it, put the information you have gathered in your REMEMBER! section into another format.
Write a short information leaflet that people can carry around with them to remind them to conserve water whenever possible.

MISSION QUESTS/SUPERQUEST 4:10–4.11

Pizza delivery dilemma

Serena, our Italian friend, has got herself into a bit of trouble. Last night she attended a state banquet held by our very own Maryland 'Tex' Wordsworth, the President of the United States. At the banquet, Serena told Tex that Italian pizzas were far better than American ones as the dough bases were thinner and crispier. Tex said that he preferred the bases thicker and with more cheese.

Serena said she would prove Italian pizzas were better. She told Tex she would supply the whole of the White House staff with an Italian pizza and they could decide which was best.

There are two small problems to overcome.

One, Serena can't cook. Two, by the time the pizzas arrive at the White House they will be cold.

Da Vinci, with your Italian genes you know I'm correct! Can you help?

She isn't going to back down now – it is time to call the Academy!

I can, Serena, so long as I get a slice of the action with extra mozzarella cheese! I'll get Echo to help. She knows all about good food.

Research Area

- Pizza dough is a form of bread dough. Explore the range of breads and pizzas. If possible, bring some different types of breads to school. Smell them, name them and talk about their texture and how you eat them.

    Look at these websites for more ideas and information:
    http://www.italianfoodforever.com
    http://www.flourandgrain.com

- Gather a collection of cookbooks in your classroom. Research different pizza toppings. A basic pizza will have fresh basil, mozzarella cheese and tomatoes (green, white and red like the Italian flag). This is called a 'Margarita'. Use the internet to find out why it has this name.

- Investigate other pizza names. What toppings do they have? Why are they given these names and do the ingredients represent anything in particular?

- The pizzas you make will need to stay warm. Revise your work on insulation. Which materials would make a good insulator for a pizza?

I'm getting hungry. Let's start cooking!

The Super Quest

First we need a basic pizza dough recipe.
Use the internet to find one of your choice. Enter 'Italian pizza dough recipe' into the search engine.
There is a good recipe at:
http://bbc.co.uk/food/recipes/database/pizza_67163.shtml

Once you have made the base, you will need the toppings.
Here is a list of tasty and healthy toppings:

- Mushrooms
- Spinach
- Olives
- Shellfish
- Peppers
- Egg
- Tuna
- Salami
- Onions
- Sweetcorn
- Anchovies
- Pepperoni

Combine any of these or use your own favourites.
Follow a recipe in one of the recipe books or from the internet.
Take care when handling food: always wash your hands before touching raw ingredients and after handling any raw meat or fish.
Be careful when working near a hot oven. Ask your teacher to help you get your pizza in and out of the oven!

Thanks, Echo. While you've been cooking, I've made this pizza box.

You can make a pizza box too.

- Copy this net onto thick card. Make sure the square is bigger than the pizza.
- Cut out the net and stick the sides together.
- Which material could you place inside the box to insulate the pizza and keep it warm?

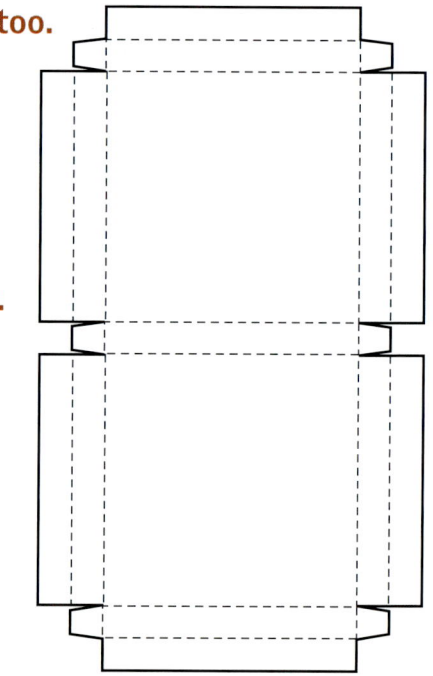

Da Vinci Files

Can you find out when the first pizza delivery company was established? How many takeaway pizzas do you think are sold each day in Great Britain?

- Use the information you find out about takeaway pizzas to research the different businesses in your area that sell pizzas.
- Do the companies try to persuade you that American or Italian pizzas are best?
- What could they do differently to convince you to buy from their restaurant?
- Gather a selection of adverts and menus for research.

Design a pizza delivery service logo that represents either American or Italian pizza styles. Write a menu and make up some new names for the pizzas that you are selling!

Now where's my moped? Tex and his pals will have a pizza party to remember. Delicioso!

Fresh PIZZA Baked!

MISSION QUEST 4:12

Grand designs

The Academy needs livening up. It's looking very drab. Can't we give it a coat of paint?

I've been going to an evening art class, Da Vinci. What about a few pictures instead? We could do something really exciting.

Sounds interesting, Mrs T. Let's get the Academy to help.

The Quest

Your quest is to choose a famous painting and reproduce it on a larger scale for the Brain Academy ballroom. In order to help you decide what might suit the Academy, gather together a collection of art magazines and journals. Ask your teachers or parents for books and postcards which show well-known and less well-known works of art.

Research Area

Start by looking at the National Gallery website at:
http://www.nationalgallery.org.uk
Visit the Tate Gallery at:
http://www.tate.org.uk   You can also follow the links to the Tate Modern, Tate Liverpool and Tate St Ives.

There is more information on pages 46–47.

The Brief

Choose a painting or work of art that you like and think would be suitable for display within the Brain Academy.
- Make a photocopy or cut out the picture. You are going to reproduce this image on a larger scale.
- Choose what you are going to put your enlargement onto. It might be:
  A large piece of paper or several pieces taped together.
  A board or flat piece of wood.
  An internal or external wall. This must be agreed to by the owner of the wall.

- Use the appropriate paints for each surface. Check the resources you need with your teacher.
- Using a ruler and pencil, draw a grid over your copy of the picture. Make sure there are good sized squares in your grid. If you are drawing on A4 paper then 5cm x 5cm should be about right.
- Now draw the same grid on the surface you are copying onto. Scale the grid up to the size you require.
- Sketch the image onto your surface using the squares to help you. You may wish to use chalk or soft pencil. Duplicate the contents of each square in as much detail as you can and make sure you step back to check that your image is accurately copied.
- When you are happy with the sketch, complete the detail on your painting with paints or pastels.

You could do this as a class activity. Each person could paint one of the squares on the grid. Join them altogether to complete the picture.

Da Vinci Files

A painting on a wall is called a mural. If you choose to do one, and it is too big for a grid, you could project the picture onto the wall using an overhead projector.
You can then trace the outline of the picture and fill in the detail. Ask your parents if you could have a mural in your bedroom. Look at http://www.littlemonkeymurals.com for some ideas on how to do it.

MISSION QUEST 4:13

Invasion games

Sandy, it's time for the annual police versus firefighters rugby match.

But we don't like playing rugby, Buster, and you guys don't like playing football.

Why don't we make up our own invasion game? Something which both our teams will enjoy. Let's ask the Academy to help us.

The Quest

Your quest is to invent a new invasion game that can be played at Brain Academy and at your school. You will need to research the definition of an 'invasion game' and decide what would be a suitable set of tactics for a game that both Buster and Sandy will enjoy playing.

Research Area

Look at existing invasion games. Football and rugby are two. Make a list of as many as you can find.

There is more information on pages 46–47.

The Brief

You will need to think about the following things when devising your new game:

- Is it an indoor game, an outdoor game or both?
- What sort of playing area is required?
- If it is a team game, how many players are there in each team?
- The purpose of football is to score more goals than the other team. What is the purpose of your game?
- What equipment is needed?
- Do the players have to wear any special clothing?
- What will you call your game?
- Think about the rules of your game:
  Is it a non-contact game?
  Is there a time limit to the game?
  Do you need a referee or umpire?
  Does the playing surface need marked areas?
- Write a rulebook for your new game.
- If possible, test the game by playing it with your friends.

It is said that rugby was invented by a schoolboy called William Webb-Ellis. Research his story on the internet.

In Tudor times, a version of football was played between entire villages. It was banned for a while! Can you find out why?

Da Vinci Files

When you have devised your game and tested it, find out if people enjoyed playing it. Implement changes to make the game better if necessary, then organise a tournament within your year or whole school.

- Invent and name a trophy to play for.
- You could have a straight knockout competition or mini-league type competition.
- Invite a neighbouring school to join in or invite them to send a team over to play.
- Make sure they understand the rules and have a chance to practise!

MISSION QUEST 4:14

What's the news?

"I love listening to the radio but I really think the standard of news programmes is falling, Buster."

"Yes, I'm on the same wavelength, Da Vinci. We could probably do much better if we made our own broadcast."

"Great idea, we could call it BARP: Brain Academy Radio Player!"

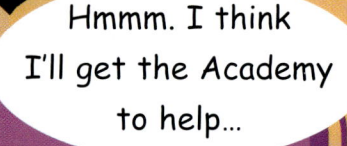

"Hmmm. I think I'll get the Academy to help…"

The Quest

Your quest is to make a radio news programme to be aired on BARP radio.

- Make notes on how the programmes are put together. What do the bulletins start with? When are the sports sections read out? When is the weather forecast transmitted?
- Listen to how newscasters read the news. What tone of voice do they use for different types of story? There is more to making a news bulletin than you might first think!

Research Area

Listen to local and national radio bulletins.
Visit the BBC website at http://www.bbc.co.uk
Collect a variety of school, local and national newspapers.

There is more information on pages 46–47.

The Brief

You could do this quest on your own or with a group of friends. Alternatively, it could be a whole class activity and form the basis of an assembly. You will need a tape recorder and microphone.

- Decide whether your programme is going to be about school news, local news or national news.
- Choose your leading story: the 'main headline'.
- Choose four or five other stories and rank them in order of importance.
- Choose a sporting headline to record.
- Add a weather forecast.
- Finish your bulletin with a light-hearted story.
- Compose your own theme tune or 'jingle' for your bulletin.
- Draft your script and edit it until it reads fluently.
- Practise reading your script at an even pace and in the style of a newsreader.
- Record your bulletin. Play it back to yourself. Rerecord it until you get it right.

Find the same story in three different newspapers. Do they give you the same information? Is there a different editorial 'slant' in the different versions that you are reading?

What differences can you find between news bulletins on Radio One and the news on Radio Four?

Da Vinci Files

- Become a TV producer! If you have access to a digital camcorder, work with a partner or group of friends to film your own news programme.
- Use props such as furniture, maps, lights and costume and make-up to help you make it as realistic as possible.
- Invite a 'live' audience to your broadcast when you record it or perform your broadcast to the class.

MISSION QUEST 4:15

Buy! Sell!

"Huxley, I've inherited £1 million from Great Uncle Harry Barrington, or Old 'Hazza' as he was known. More money is not much use to me though."

"Then you need to invest it so that it can grow and the profits can be used for your worthy causes, Bazza."

"I don't know a thing about finance. I need some help! Let's ask the Questers."

The Quest

Your quest is to invest (an imaginary!) £1 million in the London stock market and make Prince Barrington a profit for his worthy causes. You will need to look at the financial pages of the newspapers and ask your parents or teachers about the stock market and buying shares.

Research Area

The Times newspaper has a full list of all the shares available. They are listed in categories such as 'retail' or 'natural resources'.

Look at this website http://www.younginvestor.com
It is an American site but it explains the principles of investing very clearly.
http://uk.finance.yahoo.com/ is an excellent site for keeping track of shares.

There is more information on pages 46–47.

The Brief

Your teacher or an adult will need to start you off on this quest.

You must choose ten companies to invest £1 million in. This will be your 'portfolio'. To keep it manageable invest £100,000 in each one. Think about:
- Which sectors the companies you may be interested in fall under: Software, Leisure, Oil and Gas, etc.
- Which companies have you heard of? Look out for names like BP, Next, HMV, Manchester United, Alliance & Leicester.
- Look at how much the companies are selling each share for. Is the price going up or down? Look at the history of the prices. Do they follow any long-term trends?

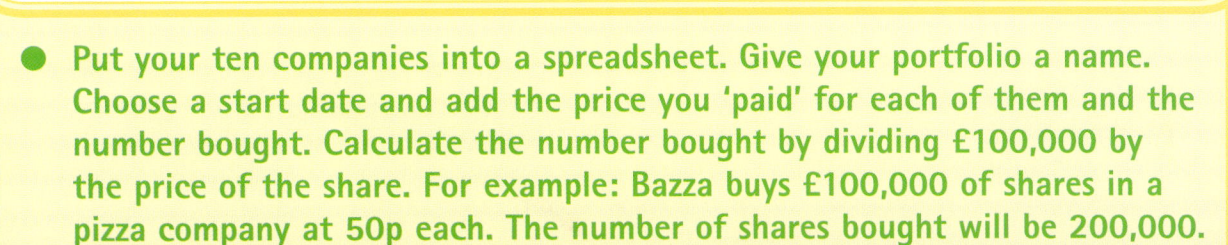

- Put your ten companies into a spreadsheet. Give your portfolio a name. Choose a start date and add the price you 'paid' for each of them and the number bought. Calculate the number bought by dividing £100,000 by the price of the share. For example: Bazza buys £100,000 of shares in a pizza company at 50p each. The number of shares bought will be 200,000.
- Check the price of your shares every day. Use the newspapers and the internet. (The yahoo finance site is the easiest to use.)
- Work out the value of your portfolio each day or at regular intervals. Do this by multiplying the number of shares you have in a company by its current price. Then add all ten company values together. Are you in profit or making a loss? You could choose a date in the future where you have to sell, which could be the end of term.

I've heard of 'Bull' and 'Bear' markets but I don't know what they are. Can you find out what they mean?

Da Vinci Files

- Now that you have had some practice, explore using spreadsheets to analyse the data in your portfolio.
- Experiment with different quantities and values.
- Make a glossary of financial jargon such as 'futures', 'pensions', 'FTSE 100', 'AIM' and 'blue-chip'.
- Can you find any ways to predict how the markets will move?
- Will you be able to give Bazza a return on his investment?

MISSION QUEST 4:16

A toy story

"My nephew wants a new toy for his seventh birthday but I don't know what he would like. Any ideas?"

"With your talent, Victor, you could make him something instead. Toys that move are always fun."

"Good idea, Bazza, but I wonder what he would like?"

The Quest

Your quest is to find out which type of moving toys Year Two children would like to play with and then make your own version of the type of toy that is most popular. You will need to carry out research and then design the toy so, first of all, devise a questionnaire for Year Two children. Make your questions specific so that you have a good idea how to design the moving toy. Good luck!

Research Area

Visit the museum of childhood for some great ideas and information about making toys:
http://www.vam.ac.uk/vastatic/nmc/index.html

There is more information on pages 46–47.

The Brief

Once you have analysed the information from your questionnaire responses, decide on the type of toy you will make.
- Sketch how the toy should look.
- Draw a plan of the design.
- Make a list of materials and equipment.
- Which parts of the toy will you be able to move?
- How will you make the parts move?

Here are some ideas. You could use one or a selection of the following.
- Electric motors: batteries and wire needed. Good for toy vehicles like cars and trains.
- Rubber band power: good for propellers on balsa wood aircraft or balsa wood boats.
- A gear system: many construction kits contain these. Use these for models like windmills or helicopters.
- Air power: balloon rockets or sails on a boat.
- Springs: how about a Jack-In-The-Box?
- Strings and pulleys: use these for making puppets.
- Gravity: pinball tables, parachute toys and marble runs use gravity.

Test your toy as you construct it. Is there anything you could do to improve it?
- Is your toy safe for a seven-year-old to use?
- Do the moving parts work every time they are used?

Decorate your toy to make it appealing to younger children.

My dad played with a toy called 'Super Flight Deck' when he was young. You can read all about it at http://ww.stuffwelove.co.uk See if you can make something like it!

Da Vinci files

You could design and construct your own 'soapbox racer' from old wood and a set of pram wheels. You steer by pulling on the rope. Attach a bar to place your feet on. This will increase your stability. You will need an adult to help you.

If you don't have access to the materials, design a prototype model for an improved soapbox racer and research ways to make it more streamlined and faster!

SUPERQUEST/MISSION QUEST 4:17–4:18

Gods and goddesses

"Hey Serena, I've just been reading about Greek myths and characters. Achilles was pretty cool. I'd give him 10/10 for bravery."

"Pah, I met Achilles on my time travels. He was a real bighead and he was a right kid!"

"Was Achilles a real person, Serena? I thought he was a mythical warrior in the story of The Illiad?"

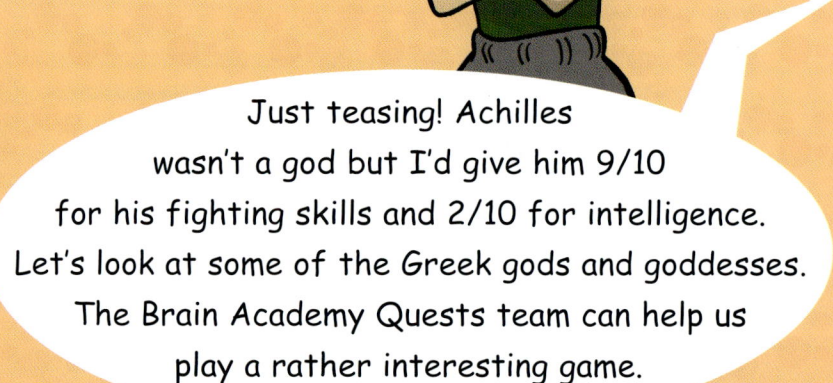

"Just teasing! Achilles wasn't a god but I'd give him 9/10 for his fighting skills and 2/10 for intelligence. Let's look at some of the Greek gods and goddesses. The Brain Academy Quests team can help us play a rather interesting game."

The Super Quest

Your quest is to research the Greek gods and goddesses and devise a card game based around their skills and attributes. Choose at least twelve Greek gods and goddesses. You could start with the twelve who lived on Mount Olympus. Study the stories behind them. What did they do? What were they like? Discuss their characters with a partner.

Research Area

Look in your school or local libraries for good books on Greek myths and legends.

Books
Illustrated Guide to Greek Myths and Legends (Usborne, ISBN 0860209466)
Horrible Histories: The Groovy Greeks (Scholastic Hippo, ISBN 0590132474)
The Orchard Book of Greek Gods and Goddesses (Orchard Books, ISBN 1860391095)

Films
Hercules (1997, Director: Ron Clements/John Musker)

http://www.factmonster.com/ipka/A0881990.html
http://www.ncl.ac.uk/shefton-museum/greeks/gods.html

There is more information on pages 46–47.

CONTINUED ➡

41

The Brief

This quest is ideal for working in pairs.

You will need the following materials:
- A blank set of playing cards or some ordinary white card.
- A black pen and colouring pencils.
- Pictures of the Greek gods and goddesses from books and the internet.
- A ruler and scissors.
- A set of 'Top Trumps' or similar card game.

Look at a card game such as 'Top Trumps'. They have categories with 'scores' or 'ratings'. The higher the scores, the higher value the card is in the game.

Make up six categories for your Greek character cards. You could use the following but feel free to choose your own:
- Strength
- Wisdom
- Cunning
- Charm
- Skills
- Popularity

REMEMBER: You will need to do a lot of research before you start attributing qualities to your cards.

- Start to rate your Greek characters with scores for each category that you have chosen.
- You could rate them out of ten or give them a percentage score. Just make sure you stick to the same method throughout.
- When you have rated each one and are happy with your selections, you are ready to make the cards.
- Each card should have the name of the character at the top, a picture of the character in the top half of the card and the scores for each category underneath.
- Draw the pictures yourself or print images from the internet and cut to size.
- When you have made your cards you are ready to play!

I wonder how many words and phrases we use today are derived from Greek heroes?

How to Play (two players)
- Deal an equal number of cards to each player.
- The person who didn't deal goes first.
- Each player looks at the top card in their hand.
- The player whose turn it is chooses a category.
- The person with the highest score wins the card and places both of the cards at the back of their pack.
- If the scores are tied, place the cards in the middle and proceed with the next card. The winner of that hand wins the cards from the previous turn as well.
- The winner is the person who wins all of the cards.

Compare your cards with ones that other people in your class have made. Are your ratings for the same characters similar?

Who was the guy holding the Earth on his shoulders? He has got to be the strongest! Can you find out more about him?

Theseus defeated the Minotaur and became a hero. But I think he was very selfish. Read the story to find out why.

Da Vinci files

You can make an 'expansion pack' for your deck.
- Research Greek heroes and make cards for the ones you find the most interesting.
- Will their ratings be less than the gods and goddesses? Maybe they will for things like 'Power' or 'Strength' but perhaps not for qualities such as 'Cunning' or 'Skills'.
- The categories should be the same as the gods and goddesses so all the cards can be used in the game.
- If your friends have made cards with the same categories as yours, you could combine the different decks to make a bigger game.
- You could also make a pack with larger cards and add a 'mini-biography' of the character on each one.
- Stylise your cards with Greek patterns and symbols such as columns and laurels.

The TASC Problem Solving Wheel
TASC: Thinking Actively in a Social Context

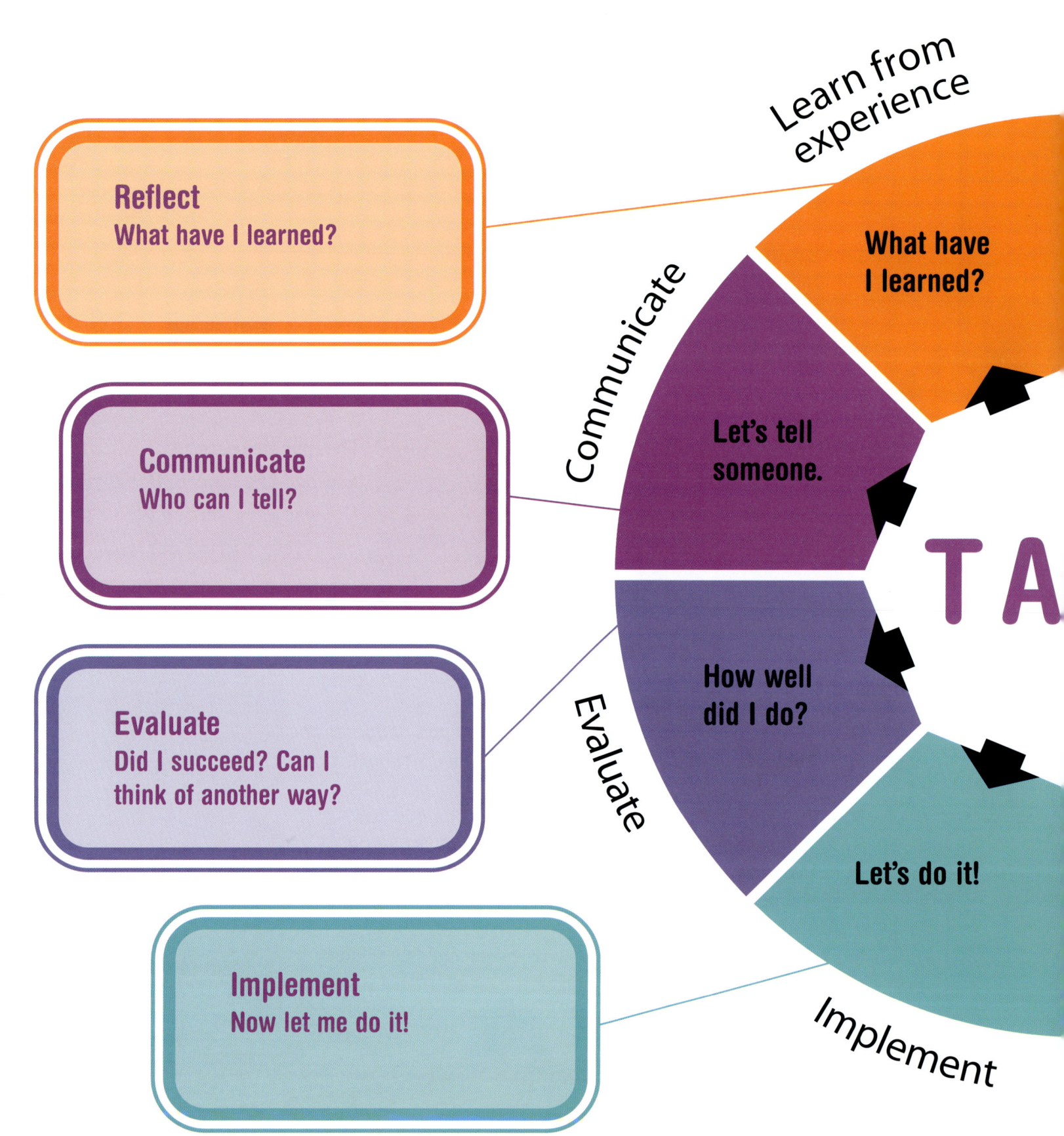

Reflect
What have I learned?

Communicate
Who can I tell?

Evaluate
Did I succeed? Can I think of another way?

Implement
Now let me do it!

Learn from experience — What have I learned?

Communicate — Let's tell someone.

Evaluate — How well did I do?

Implement — Let's do it!

We can learn to be expert thinkers!

Gather/organise
What do I know about this?

Identify
What is the task?

Generate
How many ideas can I think of?

Decide
Which is the best idea?

Gather/organise
What do I already know about this?

Identify
What am I trying to do?

Generate
How many ways can I do this?

Decide
Which is the best way?

TASC: Thinking Actively in a Social Context © Belle Wallace 2004

The Quest Online Library

MISSION QUEST 4:1
For more information try:
Book: Chambers Primary Rhyming Dictionary (Chambers, ISBN 055010089X)

MISSION QUEST 4:2
For more information try:
http://www.dltk-kids.com/world/wales/saint_david.htm
Book: Welsh for Beginners (Book and tape pack, Usborne, ISBN 074601256X)

MISSION QUEST 4:3
For more information try:
Book: Easy Peasy Sweetie Pie: Truly Scrumptious Recipes for Kids Who Love to Bake (Ebury Press, ISBN 0091877873)

MISSION QUEST 4:4
For more information try:
http://www.warwick-castle.co.uk/warwick2004/tc_timeline.htm
Book: Stephen Biesty's Cross-sections Castle (Dorling Kindersley, ISBN 1564584674)

SUPERQUEST/MISSION QUEST 4:5-4:6
For more information try:
http://www.epa.gov/globalwarming/kids
Books: the Horrible Geography range has a good selection of titles, including Stormy Weather, Perishing Poles and Desperate Deserts

MISSION QUEST 4:7
For more information try:
Book: L'ile Fantastique/Fantastic Island (Usborne, ISBN 074602373)
Book: 500 Really Useful French Words and Phrases (Hippocrene Books, ISBN 0781802679)
Learn more about children from around the world with this book: Children Just Like Me (Dorling Kindersley, ISBN 0751353272)

MISSION QUEST 4:8
For more information try the Science & Technology and Buildings & Structures sections of:
http://www.guinessworldrecords.com
http://www.crystalinks.com/seven.html
http://www.stonehenge.co.uk/history.htm

MISSION QUEST 4:9
For more information try:
http://www.kidzone.ws/water/
http://mbgnet.mobot.org/fresh/cycle/cycle.htm

SUPERQUEST/MISSION QUEST 4:10-4:11
For more information try:
http://www.dominos.uk.com/franchising/
http://www.pizzaexpress.co.uk/indexf.htm
Pizza Express runs free educational visits to their restaurants for schools. Ask your teacher if you can email them for more information: schools@pizzaexpress.com

MISSION QUEST 4:12
http://en.wikipedia.org/wiki/Mural
Look for murals near where you live. Shopping centres, subways and tube and train stations are often decorated with colourful murals that celebrate the local area.

MISSION QUEST 4:13
For more information try:
http://news.bbc.co.uk/sportacademy/
Books: look up the subject you are interested in learning about in one of the Know the Game books (Stackpole Books)

MISSION QUEST 4:14
For more information try:
http://www.takeoverradio.org/pages/takeoverradio.htm
http://news.bbc.co.uk/cbbcnews/default.stm

MISSION QUEST 4:15
For more information try:
http://news.bbc.co.uk/1/hi/business/default.stm has useful information on how business works.
Put the name of the company you are investing in into your search engine and view its company report.

MISSION QUEST 4:16
For more information try:
http://www.hitchams.suffolk.sch.uk/schoolwork/moving_toys.htm
Investigate a moving toy of your own. Look at sets of instructions for construction toys or ones that you have built yourself from a kit.

SUPERQUEST/MISSION QUEST 4:17-4:18
For more information try:
http://www.mythweb.com/
Books: The Iliad by Homer (Penguin Classics, ISBN 0140447946)
The Odyssey by Homer (Penguin Classics, ISBN 0140449116)

What is NACE?

NACE is a charity which was set up in 1984. It is an organisation that supports the teaching of 'more-able' pupils and helps all children find out what they are good at and to do their best.

What does NACE do?

NACE helps teachers by giving them advice, books, materials and training. Many teachers, headteachers, parents and governors join NACE. Members of NACE can use a special website which gives them useful advice, ideas and materials to help children to learn.

NACE helps thousands of schools and teachers every year. It also helps teachers and children in other countries, such as America and China.

How will this book help me?

Brain Academy books challenge and help you to become better at learning by:
- Thinking of and testing different solutions to problems
- Making connections to what you already know
- Making mistakes and learning from them
- Working with your teacher, by yourself and with others
- Expecting you to get better and to go on to the next book
- Learning skills which you can use in other subjects and out of school.

We hope that you enjoy the books!

Write to **RISING STARS** and let us know how the books helped you to learn and what you would like to see in the next books.

RISING STARS

Rising Stars UK Ltd, 22 Grafton Street, London W1S 4EX